Who Pooped? in the Park

Written by Steve Kemp
Illustrated by Robert Rath

FARCOUNTRY
PRESS

ISBN 10: 1-56037-321-0
ISBN 13: 978-1-56037-321-6

© 2005 by Farcountry Press
Based on a story by Gary D. Robson
Illustrations © 2005 by Robert Rath

For more information about our books, write Farcountry Press, P.O. Box 5630, Helena, MT 59604;
call (800) 821-3874; or visit www.farcountrypress.com.

CIP data is on file at the Library of Congress.

Manufactured by
Versa Press, Inc.
Spring Bay Road/Route 26
East Peoria, IL 61611-9788
in November 2014

Book design by Robert Rath.
Produced and printed in the United States of America.

18 17 16 15 14   5 6 7 8 9

"We made it. We're really in the
Great Smoky Mountains," Grant said.

"I hope we see some animals!" said Julie.

"I want to see a bear!" said Grant.
"Dad said we'd see lots of wildlife."

3

"What a beautiful view of the
Great Smoky Mountains," Mom said.

"Pretty," Julie said.

4

"How come we haven't seen any animals yet?" said Grant.

"It seems like we should have seen some animals by now," Grant said.
"All I see are trees."

"If Dad said we'd see wildlife, I'm sure we'll see some," Julie assured him.

"Hey, look, there's a wildlife walk today," Dad said.

"Can we do that?" Grant and Julie said, almost in unison.

"Hi, my name is Ranger Gus.
Are you coming on the walk today?"
the ranger said.

"Will we see animals?" Grant asked.

"That depends," Ranger Gus said.

"Depends on what?" Grant asked.

"It depends on whether or not you
know how to look," Ranger Gus said.

ONE
MILE
LOOP

"Grant, what are you doing?" Julie asked.

"Practicing looking for bears," said Grant.

"What's that?" said Julie.

"A clue," said Ranger Gus.

"It kind of looks like candy," Grant said.

"It does look a little like candy,
but it's not. It's scat," said Ranger Gus.

10

"What's *scat*?"
Grant asked.

"Poop," said Ranger Gus.
"Scat is another word for
wild animal poop."

"Who pooped, I mean scatted, here?" asked Grant.

"I think it's a cottontail rabbit," said Ranger Gus, "but let's look around for more clues to be sure."

"See here where the little fellow has been resting?" said Gus. "A nice comfy bed just the size of a rabbit."

"And here he's had a bite to eat. See how he's nipped off the twig at an angle? That's a rabbit clue, too."

"See here in the mud?" Ranger Gus said. "We've been right all along. These are rabbit tracks. See the long back feet and smaller, round front feet?"

"Wow, you can find lots of clues if you know how to look," said Grant.

the STRAIGHT POOP

Rabbits sometimes eat their own scat! They do this in order to get as much nutrition from their food as they can. The small round pellets you find are food that has been digested twice.

"Look, Ranger Gus," said Julie.
"Super big rabbit scat."

"Wow," said Grant. "That rabbit must
be as big as the Easter Bunny."

"It does look like rabbit scat,
but it's too big for a rabbit,"
said Ranger Gus. "Let's look
for more clues."

"I found some tracks!" said Julie. "Big ones!"

"Good work," said Ranger Gus. "You've found hoof prints. See how it's made up of two parts? Judging by the size of the tracks and scat, I'd say we're seeing a white-tailed deer."

"Mom, Dad, we found deer tracks and scat!" yelled Julie.

the STRAIGHT POOP

Before the Great Smoky Mountains became protected as a national park, most of the white-tailed deer had been killed or chased away. Now they are common in places like Cades Cove.

"And judging from this other clue, it's a male deer." said Gus.

"How can you tell that, Ranger Gus?" Grant asked.

"See where the bark's been scraped on this young tree?" Ranger Gus said.
"Male deer do that with their antlers to let other deer know they live here."

the STRAIGHT POOP

Male deer are called bucks, female deer are called does, and baby deer are called fawns.

"Hey, Ranger Gus," Grant said. "Some deer really marked this tree."

"Whoa," said Julie, "he really wanted other deer to know his address."

"Maybe he was expecting a letter?" Grant said.

"I think we're seeing a different animal now," said Ranger Gus. "I don't think antlers scraped this tree, I think it was done with teeth. Let's find more clues."

"Look, lots more chewed trees," Julie said.

"Yes, and look at this dam," Ranger Gus said. "Beavers cut down trees to build dams and to get the bark and buds to eat. You see, beavers can't climb trees, so they bring the tasty twigs and branches down to their level. The dams create ponds where beavers can escape from predators."

the STRAIGHT
POOP

Beavers poop in the water, so you almost never see their scat.

"So, these must be beaver tracks, too," said Julie.

"Duh!" said Grant.

"Good guess, kids," said Ranger Gus, "but beavers don't often
leave tracks. They drag their flat tails behind them, and that rubs
out their tracks. I think these belong to another animal."

"Their tracks are similar to dog tracks, like Labrador retrievers. You can see their claw marks."

"Hey, I found some scat," said Grant.

"Good work," said Ranger Gus. "And if I'm not mistaken, it was made by the same animals as the tracks we just found. The coyote."

the STRAIGHT POOP

Coyote scat often contains hair from the animals (mice, rabbits, squirrels, groundhogs, etc.) it has eaten.

"Ranger Gus," Julie said. "This is really strange. Look how all the leaves are fluffed up over here."

"Hmmm," said Ranger Gus. "It looks to me like some animal has been scraping away the leaves and looking for bugs and acorns to eat. Any other clues around here?"

"Look! Look! I found poop," said Grant, proudly.

"Scat," said Julie and Gus.

"So far every animal we've discovered has been a mammal," said Ranger Gus. "But this isn't. I think we're seeing a bird."

the STRAIGHT POOP

Mammals are a class of animals. They have these things in common:

- most are hairy
- warm blooded
- mothers feed milk to their babies

"Wow, look at the size of these bird tracks!"
exclaimed Julie.

"By gosh, it's a wild turkey," said Ranger Gus.
"From the looks of it, a whole flock has been feeding here."

the STRAIGHT POOP

Male wild turkeys measure nearly four feet from beak to tail. Females are about three feet long.

"Hey, Ranger Gus," said Grant. "Look at this little hole in the ground. Did a bear do this?"

"Well," said Gus. "I do believe another of our forest friends has been digging bugs and grubs. Maybe if we use our noses we can figure out who it is."

"P.U." said Grant.

"Something died," said Julie.

"And if you look closely at the scat,"
Ranger Gus said, "you can see the wings
and legs of the insects it's been eating."

31

"I know," said Julie. "It's a skunk!"

"See the tiny tracks?" said Ranger Gus. "Five toes, just like us. And long claws for digging bugs and grubs."

the STRAIGHT POOP

Skunks can spray a very smelly liquid ten feet with pinpoint accuracy. The over-powering odor may last for weeks.

"Weird," said Grant. "Why is everything so stirred up here?"

"It looks like the garden after mom and dad dig it up with the tiller," said Julie.

"This is quite a find," said Ranger Gus. "We've happened upon an alien to the Great Smoky Mountains."

"An alien garden tiller?" asked Grant.

"Not quite, Grant," Ranger Gus laughed.

the STRAIGHT POOP

Wild hogs are native to Europe. When Ranger Gus calls them alien, he means they are not native to the Great Smokies, they were brought in from somewhere else.

"Here's a track and some scat," said Julie.

"Just as I thought," said Ranger Gus. "See how the track is a hoof, kind of like a deer? No ifs, ands, or buts; we're seeing wild hogs here."

35

"Wild hogs don't belong in the Smokies," said Ranger Gus. "They escaped from a hunting preserve long ago and moved into the park. Wild hogs are very destructive. They dig up the ground with their snouts, hurt our wildflowers, and eat our salamanders."

the STRAIGHT POOP

Wild hogs weigh as much as 300 pounds. Rangers trap them and remove them from the park so they don't do so much damage.

"Well, our hike's almost over," said Ranger Gus. "Did you enjoy the walk?"

"I sure did," said Julie. "You showed us how to figure out what animals are around by the clues they leave behind."

"I only wish we could have seen a bear, too," said Grant.

"A bear, eh?" said Ranger Gus. "Why didn't you say so? There's a side path down to the river here that bears sometimes use."

"Hey, somebody moved this big rock," said Julie.

"I'd say a bear did that," said Ranger Gus. "It was looking for food."

"Whoa! This rock is heavy," said Grant.

"That shows you how strong a bear is," said Ranger Gus.

"Look, tracks," said Julie.
"But it looks like a barefoot person."

"It does look like a human foot,
but it's not," said Ranger Gus.
"The hind footprint of a bear
looks much like a human footprint."

41

"Look out, Ranger Gus!"
Julie cried out. "You're
about to step in…"

the STRAIGHT POOP

Smoky Mountain black bears eat mostly berries, acorns, nuts, leaves, and insects.

If you find hair in their scat, they've been eating animals such as mice, woodchucks, or deer.

"Bear poop!" said Grant.

"Bear *scat*," said Ranger Gus. "I should have been paying more attention to where I was stepping! Anyway, look at all the seeds. Our bear has sure been eating lots of berries."

43

"Look, kids, there's a bear!" said Ranger Gus.
"If we keep our distance, it may let us watch for a while."

"Cool!" exclaimed Grant. "Thanks for showing us the bear
and all the other animals!"

"All in a day's work," said Ranger Gus.

"I want to be a ranger when I grow up!" said Julie.

TRACKS and SCAT NOTES

COTTONTAIL RABBIT

Back feet are long and narrow; front feet are oval.

Scat is small round balls.

WHITE-TAILED DEER

Tracks are pairs of hooves about as long as your thumb.

Scat is twenty to thirty oval pellets, each about the size of a jellybean.

BEAVER

Tracks and scat are seldom seen. Signs of beavers include obviously gnawed tree stumps and dams.

COYOTE

Tracks are dog-like. Claws often show.

Scat is long and may be pointed at the end.

WILD TURKEY

Turkey tracks are four to five inches long.

Turkey scat is often green and either curled or J-shaped.

SKUNK

Tracks show five toes with small claw marks in front of each.

Scat is usually black and contains insect parts, berry seeds, and sometimes rodent hair.

WILD HOG

Tracks show hooves similar to deer tracks, but the two parts are farther apart.

Scat is tubular.

BLACK BEAR

Back feet are six to seven inches long. Front feet are four inches long and four inches wide.

Scat can be piles or large tubes, depending on what the bear has been eating.

ABOUT the AUTHORS

STEVE KEMP worked as a seasonal park ranger in Yellowstone and Denali national parks and has been employed by Great Smoky Mountains Association as a writer, editor, and Interpretive Products and Services Director since 1987. He wrote the text for George Humphries' photography book *Great Smoky Mountain Impressions* and for *Great Smoky Mountains Simply Beautiful*, a collection of photography by Adam Jones; Steve is also the author of *Trees of the Smokies*. He has written articles for *Outdoor Life*, *Outside*, *National Parks*, *Outdoor Photographer*, and the Discovery Channel guidebook series.

ROBERT RATH is a book designer and illustrator living in Bozeman, Montana. Although he has worked with Scholastic Books, Lucasfilm, and Montana State University, his favorite project is keeping up with his family. This book is dedicated to his two poop experts, Lucy and Thomas.